GEORGE FOREMAN®

GRILLING PLAYBOOK

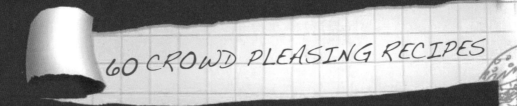

60 CROWD PLEASING RECIPES

sausages

chicken

baguett

© 2012 Applica Consumer Products, Inc.

Published in the United States of America by:

Applica Consumer Products, Inc.

Miramar, FL 33027

© 2012 Applica Consumer Products, Inc.

ISBN: 978-0-615-63730-3

9 8 7 6 5 4 3 2

Printed in the United States of America.

LET'S GET THIS PARTY STARTED!

George Foreman® grill fans love to entertain family and friends with delicious recipes hot off the grill! Enjoy the recipes in this book to help you serve up your next winning meal; from sideline snacks for a junior league tournament to a sweet, post-win dessert celebration.
For the best results, review the pregame prep notes on pages 2 to 4.

GO TEAM!
George Foreman Cooking Team

TRAINING CAMP

BREAKFAST

APPETIZERS

TABLE *of* CONTENTS

CALL A
TIME-OUT
for FUN!

Warm-Up Your Grill *for* the Big Day

1. If using a grill with removable plates, attach the appropriate plates based on your selected recipe using the release handles. If using a fixed plate grill review steps 2 and 4.

2. When using grill plates, tilt the grill by adjusting the lever at the back of the grill and place the drip tray below the front of the grill. Note: Not all grills can be adjusted. Standard grills are already in a sloped position.

3. When using a bake/pizza/griddle plate, adjust the lever at the back of the grill so that the grill is flat. The drip tray is not used when using the bake plate.

4. Select the desired cooking temperature and preheat the grill.
   When the ready indicator light changes, the grill is ready for use.

5. Consult your grill's Use and Care manual for more detailed instructions.

GRILLING TIPS from the Playbook

- To prevent heat loss and for even cooking, do not open the lid frequently.

- When cooking several pieces of food, try to have them similar in size and thickness.

- Remember that since the grill is cooking from both sides, the cooking time will typically be shorter than expected. Watch carefully to avoid overcooking.

* __Important__: Use only silicone, plastic and wooden utensils when cooking on the grill.

GRILLING GUIDE

FOOD	COOKING TIME	TEMPERATURE SETTING	COMMENTS
Beef, Pork & Lamb			
Fresh Hamburger (5 oz.)	4-6 minutes	High	3/4-inch thick Cooked to medium (160°F)
Frozen Hamburger (5 oz.)	5-6 minutes	High	3/4-inch thick Cooked to medium (160°F)
Flank Steak (3/4 lb.)	6-8 minutes	High	3/4-inch thick Cooked to medium rare (145°F)
Skirt Steak (1/2 lb.)	4-6 minutes	High	3/4-inch thick Cooked to medium (160°F)
NY Strip Steak (shell steak) (6 oz.)	6-8 minutes	High	3/4-inch thick Cooked to medium rare (145°F)
Beef Tenderloin (5 oz.)	4-6 minutes	High	3/4-inch thick Cooked to medium rare (145°F)
Beef Kabobs	5-7 minutes	High	Cooked to medium (160°F)
Pork Loin Chops, boneless	4-6 minutes	Medium High	3/4-inch thick Cooked to 160°F
Pork Loin Chops, bone in	4-6 minutes	Medium High	1/2-inch thick Cooked to 160°F
Sausage, Link or Patty	4-6 minutes	Medium High	Cooked to 160°F
Hot Dogs	4-5 minutes	Medium High	Cooked to 168°
Bacon	6-8 minutes	Medium High	Cook until crisp
Smoked Pork Loin Chops, boneless	4-6 minutes	Medium High	Cooked to 160°F
Lamb Loin Chops	5-7 minutes	High	3/4-inch thick Cooked to medium (160°F)

FOOD	COOKING TIME	TEMPERATURE SETTING	COMMENTS
Chicken & Turkey			
Chicken Breast, boneless and skinless (8 oz.)	11-13 minutes	Medium High	Cooked to 170°
Chicken Tenderloins 4 to 6 pieces	4-6 minutes	Medium High	Cooked to 170°
Turkey Tenderloin (1/2 lb.)	9-11 minutes	Medium High	Cooked to 170°
Turkey Burgers (5 oz.)	4-6 minutes	Medium High	Cooked to 170°

FOOD

Fish

Food	Cooking Time	Temperature Setting	Comments
Tilapia Fillets (6 oz., ea.)	5-7 minutes	Medium	Cooked to 145°F
Trout Fillet (6 oz.)	4-6 minutes	Medium	Cooked to 145°F
Salmon Fillet (8 oz., ea.)	5-7 minutes	Medium	Cooked to 145°F
Salmon Steak (6-8 oz.)	7-9 minutes	Medium High	Cooked to 145°F
Tuna Steak (6 oz.)	4-6 minutes	Medium High	Cooked to 145°F
Shrimp	3-4 minutes	Medium High	Cooked to 145°F

FOOD

Sandwiches

Food	Cooking Time	Temperature Setting	Comments
Grilled Cheese	2-3 minutes	Medium	Cook until cheese is melted and sandwich is golden
Grilled Cheese with tomato, tuna, ham or bacon	3-4 minutes	Medium	Cook until cheese is melted and sandwich is golden
Quesadillas	2-3 minutes	Medium	Cook until cheese is melted and tortilla is lightly browned

FOOD

Fruits & Vegetables

Food	Cooking Time	Temperature Setting	Comments
Asparagus Spears	4-6 minutes	Medium High	
Bell Peppers, assorted colors cut into 1/2-inch rings	5-7 minutes	Medium High	
Mushrooms, thickly sliced	4-5 minutes	Medium High	
Onion Slices, 1/2-inch	5-7 minutes	Medium High	
Potato Slices, 1/2-inch	15-18 minutes	Medium High	
Portabella Mushrooms, 3-inch diameter	4-6 minutes	Medium High	
Zucchini Slices, 1/2-inch	3-4 minutes	Medium High	
Fresh Pineapple Slices	2-4 minutes	Medium High	
Banana Slices	3-4 minutes	Medium High	

CROISSANT FRENCH TOAST
with Warm Berries (page 9)

BREAKFAST SANDWICH
page 15 ↘

Plates needed: Top Grilling Plate; Bottom Bake Plate
Preheat temperature: High
Estimated cooking time: 3 minutes

servings **4**

Oatmeal Cinnamon Raisin Pancakes

INGREDIENTS

1¼ cups	**buttermilk** divided
1 cup	**quick-cooking old-fashioned oats** (not instant)
1 cup	**unsifted all-purpose flour**
3 tablespoons	**dark brown sugar**
1 ½ teaspoons	**baking powder**
1 teaspoon	**ground cinnamon**
1 teaspoon	**ground nutmeg**
½ teaspoon	**baking soda**
2	**eggs** lightly beaten
⅓ cup	**low-fat margarine** melted
1 teaspoon	**vanilla extract**
½ cup	**raisins**

DIRECTIONS

1. In a small bowl, combine oats and 1-cup buttermilk. Stir to blend and let stand for 10 minutes.

2. In a large bowl, combine the oat mixture with the remaining ingredients, except the raisins. Stir to mix well.

3. Add the raisins and stir just to blend.

4. Spoon the batter onto the preheated baking plate using a ¼-cup measuring cup.

5. Close lid and cook the pancakes for 3 minutes or until browned and the edges are slightly dry.

6. Keep warm in an oven set at 250°F or serve immediately with syrup or honey.

7. Allow grill to reheat. Repeat with the remaining batter.

Plates needed: Top Grilling Plate; Bottom Bake Plate
Preheat temperature: Medium
Estimated cooking time: 15 minutes

Easy Cinnamon Raisin Roll-ups

INGREDIENTS

1 tablespoon	sugar
¼ teaspoon	ground cinnamon
	generous dash ground nutmeg
1	8-ounce package refrigerated crescent rolls
2 tablespoons	melted butter or margarine
¼ cup	chopped pecans
2 tablespoons	raisins
	powdered sugar

DIRECTIONS

1. In small bowl, mix the sugar, cinnamon and nutmeg; blend well.

2. Unroll dough and separate into 8 triangles. Brush the top of each triangle with melted butter.

3. Sprinkle the dough evenly with the sugar mixture. Top with nuts and raisins. Roll up crescents loosely. Arrange in preheated bake plate.

4. Bake until golden on top and fully baked internally. Remove bake plate from grill and let cool in bake plate for 10 minutes.

5. Sprinkle with powdered sugar before serving.

Tip from the Playbook

Kick-off your day with BREAKFAST

Plates needed: Grilling Plates
Preheat temperature: High
Estimated cooking time: 10 minutes

servings **4**

Croissant French Toast with Warm Berries

INGREDIENTS

½ cup	fresh blackberries
½ cup	fresh blueberries
½ cup	fresh raspberries
¼ cup	sugar
1 tablespoon	cornstarch
2 tablespoons	cold water
½ teaspoon	vanilla extract
¾ cup	liquid egg substitute
¼ cup	low-fat milk
½ teaspoon	almond extract
4	large croissants
	halved lengthwise
	powdered sugar

DIRECTIONS

1. In a small saucepan, combine the berries and sugar and bring to a boil. Reduce heat to low.

2. Whisk the cornstarch into the water until it is dissolved and then add it to the berries. Simmer for 2 minutes, stirring constantly until thickened and smooth. Remove from heat and stir in vanilla extract. Set aside and keep warm.

3. In a pie plate or shallow bowl, whisk together the egg substitute, milk and almond extract.

4. Quickly dip the croissant halves into the batter, turning to coat both sides. Do not soak the croissants because they are soft and may disintegrate.

5. Place the croissants on the preheated grill and close the lid. Cook for 3 minutes or until golden brown and heated through.

6. To serve, spoon the warm berries into the bottom half of a croissant and cover with remaining top half. Sprinkle with powdered sugar.

SEE PHOTO ↗
on page 5

6
POINTS

servings **4**

Plates needed: Grilling Plates
Preheat temperature: Medium High
Estimated cooking time: 3-4 minutes

Grilled Bananas

INGREDIENTS

2 **ripe bananas**
peeled

2 tablespoons **sugar**

½ teaspoon **cinnamon**

2 tablespoons **walnuts or pecans**
finely chopped

DIRECTIONS

1. Cut the bananas in half horizontally and vertically

2. In a small bowl, combine the sugar, cinnamon and walnuts.

3. Place the bananas on the preheated grill horizontally and spoon the walnut mixture over each slice.

4. Grill 3 minutes, or until the bananas are warm and slightly glazed.

BREAKFAST

Plates needed: Top Grilling Plate; Bottom Bake Plate
Preheat temperature: Medium
Estimated cooking time: 20 minutes

servings
6 (12 biscuits)

Fresh Home-Baked Biscuits

INGREDIENTS

2 cups	unsifted all-purpose flour
2½ teaspoons	baking powder
½ teaspoon	salt
5 tablespoons	cold low-fat margarine cut into pieces
¾ cup	low-fat milk

DIRECTIONS

1. In a large bowl, mix the flour, baking powder and salt. Using a pastry blender or 2 knives, cut the margarine into the flour mixture until it resembles coarse crumbs.

2. Make a well in the center of the flour mixture and pour in the milk. Gently stir with a fork until the dough forms a mass.

3. Gather the dough and shape it into a ball on a lightly floured surface. Knead the dough, pulling the edges to the center and pushing it into itself about 5 times. The dough will feel light and soft, but not sticky.

4. Roll the dough into a circle about ¼ inch thick.

5. Using a 2 to 3-inch round cookie cutter, cut out circles as close together as possible.

6. Place about 6 biscuits on a preheated baking plate, 1-inch apart.

7. Close lid and bake for 6 to 8 minutes, until the biscuits are puffed and golden brown.

8. Allow grill to reheat. Repeat with the remaining biscuits.

1
POINTS

Plates needed: Grilling Plates
Preheat temperature: High
Estimated cooking time: 4-5 minutes

Crispy Hash Brown Potatoes

INGREDIENTS

2	large russet potatoes
½ teaspoon	salt
¼ teaspoon	black pepper
2 teaspoons	extra-virgin olive oil

DIRECTIONS

1. Scrub the potatoes and grate through a food processor or with a hand grater.
2. Place the grated potatoes in a wire mesh strainer and gently press to remove all liquid.
3. Dry the potatoes well and toss with salt and pepper.
4. Place the grated potatoes in the preheated grill and spread evenly to a thickness of ¼-inch.
5. Drizzle the oil over the potatoes and close the lid.
6. Cook for 4 minutes or until potatoes are tender in the center and crispy browned on the bottom.
7. Serve immediately with applesauce or reduced fat sour cream, if desired.

BREAKFAST

Breakfast Tacos

INGREDIENTS

6	eggs
1 teaspoon	salt
¼ teaspoon	black pepper
4	large non-fat flour tortillas
2 tablespoons	low-fat margarine

Choose 2 or more of the following ingredients:

¼ cup	cooked low-fat sausage crumbled
¼ cup	cooked turkey bacon crumbled
2	green onions finely chopped
¼ cup	canned green chiles chopped
¼ cup	cooked potatoes
¼ cup	low-fat Monterey Jack cheese grated
¼ cup	low-fat longhorn cheddar cheese grated
¼ cup	prepared salsa

DIRECTIONS

1. In a medium bowl, whisk together eggs, salt and pepper. Add 2 or more ingredients from the additional list and stir to blend.

2. Place 2 tortillas in the preheated grill and heat for 40 seconds. Transfer to a plate; cover and keep warm. Repeat with remaining tortillas.

3. Place the margarine in the grill, close the lid and let the margarine melt for 30 seconds. Pour the egg mixture into the grill, close the lid and cook for 20 seconds. Open the grill and scramble well. Close the lid and cook for an additional 20 seconds or to desired doneness.

4. Divide egg mixture among the warm tortillas and roll up. If desired, garnish with additional salsa.

POINTS

Plates needed: Grilling Plates
Preheat temperature: High
Estimated cooking time: 5 minutes

Texas Style Sausage

INGREDIENTS

1	**egg white** slightly beaten
⅓ cup	**onion** finely chopped
¼ cup	**seasoned bread crumbs**
¼ cup	**green chili peppers** diced
1	**large garlic clove** minced
2 tablespoon	**fresh cilantro** chopped
1 tablespoon	**cider vinegar**
1½ teaspoon	**chili powder**
¼ teaspoon	**sea salt**
⅛ teaspoon	**cayenne pepper**
½ pound	**lean ground beef**

DIRECTIONS

1. In a medium bowl, combine all ingredients, except the ground beef, and blend well.
2. Add beef and mix well.
3. Shape mixture into 8 3-inch patties.
4. Place on the preheated grill and cook for about 3 minutes or to desired doneness.

Breakfast Sandwich

INGREDIENTS

butter

4 slices Canadian bacon

2 eggs

4 slices sharp cheddar cheese

2 slices tomato

2 english muffins
split and toasted

salt and pepper

DIRECTIONS

1. Place Canadian bacon on the bake plate on the preheated grill. Add ½ teaspoon butter to the bake pan and allow to melt.

2. Break eggs on top of the melted butter. Season with salt and pepper.

3. Close lid and cook for 2 minutes. Open grill and turn bacon over and top with cheese slices.

4. Once the eggs have set, turn them over and continue cooking to desired doneness.

5. Place Canadian bacon and slice of tomato on bottom of English muffin and place egg on top. Top with remaining half of English muffin.

SEE PHOTO
on page 6

Grilled
Bacon-Wrapped
SHRIMP
page 20 →

APPETIZERS

Thai Chicken Skewers
with Peanut Sauce
page 29

ALL-AMERICAN
Beef & Blue
Cheese Sliders
page 34

Vietnamese Lettuce-Wrapped Shrimp

INGREDIENTS

4	**8-inch wooden skewers**
16	**large shrimp**
	peeled, deveined and tails removed
1 tablespoon	**sesame oil**
1 tablespoon	**low-sodium soy sauce**
½ teaspoon	**Asian chili oil**
¼ teaspoon	**black pepper**
4	**large leaves of butter lettuce**
	rinsed and dried
2 cups	**grated carrots**
2 cups	**bean sprouts**
	rinsed and cut into 1-inch pieces
¼ cup	**hoisin sauce**

DIRECTIONS

1. Soak wooden skewers in water in a 9-inch pie plate for at least 20 minutes.

2. Remove skewers from water and thread the shrimp onto the skewers.

3. In a small bowl, combine sesame oil, soy sauce, chili oil and pepper.

4. Brush the shrimp with the oil mixture and place on preheated grill horizontally.

5. Grill the shrimp for 3 minutes or until pink and cooked through.

6. Remove the shrimp from skewers. To assemble the wraps, place the shrimp, carrots and bean sprouts on a lettuce leaf and roll up, tucking in the ends. Serve with hoisin sauce.

Tip from the Playbook

Provide your Half-time Entertainment with APPETIZERS!

POINTS

Grilled Bacon-Wrapped Shrimp

See photo on
★ pg. 16

INGREDIENTS

4 **8-inch wooden skewers**

8 **slices bacon**

16 **large shrimp**
peeled and deveined,
tails on

32 **1-inch cubes fresh
pineapple**

DIRECTIONS

1. Soak wooden skewers in water in a 9-inch pie plate for at least 20 minutes.

2. Place the bacon strips on the grill and cook for 3 minutes. Bacon should be pliable when done. Cook bacon in 2 batches if needed.

3. Remove the partially cooked bacon and place on paper towels to drain.

4. When the bacon is cool enough to handle, cut the bacon strips in half, horizontally.

5. Wrap each shrimp in a piece of bacon and thread onto the skewer, alternating with pineapple chunks. Place 4 shrimp on each skewer.

6. Place the skewers in the preheated grill horizontally, close the lid and cook for 3 minutes or until pink and cooked through.

APPETIZERS

Plates needed: Top Grilling Plate; Bottom Bake Plate
Preheat temperature: High
Estimated cooking time: 4 minutes

servings 4

Maryland Crab Cakes

INGREDIENTS

	Fresh lump crab meat or 1 6-ounce can lump crab meat
¼ cup	fine dry bread crumbs
¼ cup	low-fat mayonnaise
¼ cup	minced celery
2 teaspoons	minced fresh parsley
2 teaspoons	seafood seasoning
¼ teaspoon	black pepper
¼ teaspoon	baking powder
1	egg yolk slightly beaten
2 teaspoons	fresh lemon juice
½ teaspoon	Dijon mustard
¼ teaspoon	Worcestershire sauce
¾ cup	corn meal
1 tablespoon	canola oil

DIRECTIONS

1. In a medium bowl, gently combine all the ingredients, except corn meal and canola oil.

2. Form the mixture into 8 small ½-inch patties.

3. Pour the corn meal into a pie plate. Coat the sides of crab cakes in corn meal.

4. Place the crab cakes on a baking sheet and cover with plastic wrap. Refrigerate for at least 1 hour or overnight.

5. Drizzle 1 tablespoon of canola oil onto the baking plate.

6. Place the crab cakes on the preheated grill. Close the lid and cook for 4 minutes or until golden and cooked through.

POINTS

Plates needed: Top Grilling Plate; Bottom Bake Plate
Preheat temperature: Medium
Estimated cooking time: 10 minutes

Pigs 'n Blankets

INGREDIENTS

1   8-ounce package
    refrigerated crescent rolls

1   14-ounce package beef
    smoked sausages

    honey mustard

    ketchup

DIRECTIONS

1. Unroll the dough and separate into
    4 pieces. Pinch perforated seams
    to close. Cut into thin strips.

2. Roll up the sausages and place
    seam side down on work surface.

3. Place 16 sausages in a single
    layer in baking plate, allowing
    approximately 1-inch between
    roll-ups.

4. Cook for 10 minutes or until dough
    is golden and puffed.

5. Serve with ketchup and
    honey mustard.

Franks 'n Kraut

INGREDIENTS

1 **12-ounce package beef franks**

1 **8-ounce can sauerkraut**

hot dog buns

mustard

ketchup

DIRECTIONS

1. Brown beef franks in a preheated baking pan, turning occasionally to brown all sides.

2. Add sauerkraut to the baking plate.

3. Close lid and cook 5 minutes or until a meat thermometer inserted into the center of the beef franks registers 165°F.

4. Serve the beef franks on buns topped with sauerkraut, mustard and ketchup.

POINTS

Plates needed: Grilling Plates
Preheat temperature: High
Estimated cooking time: 3 minutes

Ham and Pineapple Sandwiches

INGREDIENTS

¼ cup	**pineapple preserves**
¼ cup	**canned peaches** chopped
1 tablespoon	**candied ginger** finely diced
2 tablespoon	**melted butter**
4	**slices sourdough bread**
4 ounces	**ham** thinly sliced
4 ounces	**brie** sliced

DIRECTIONS

1. In small bowl, mix the pineapple preserves, peaches and ginger; set aside.

2. Spread butter on one side of each slice of bread.

3. Place 2 slices of bread, buttered side down, on a cutting board. Spread the pineapple mixture onto the bread, and then top each slice of bread with ham and cheese. Cover with the remaining slices of bread, buttered side up.

4. Grill for 3 minutes or until the bread is golden and cheese is softened.

5. Cut into quarters and serve.

Plates needed: Grilling Plates
Preheat temperature: High
Estimated cooking time: 4 minutes

servings **4**

Prosciutto and Provolone Panini

INGREDIENTS

4	thick slices Italian bread
	olive oil
2 tablespoon	prepared pesto
4 ounces	thinly sliced prosciutto
½ cup	packaged roasted tomatoes
4 ounces	provolone cheese sliced

DIRECTIONS

1. Brush one side of each slice of bread with olive oil. Place the bread, olive oil brushed sides down, onto the cutting board or work surface.

2. Spread pesto on the slices of bread. Top with prosciutto, tomatoes and provolone cheese. Cover with remaining 2 slices of bread; oiled side out.

3. Cook on preheated grill for about 4 minutes or until the bread is golden and cheese is melted.

4. Cut in half and serve warm.

POINTS

Plates needed: Grilling Plates
Preheat temperature: Low
Estimated cooking time: 3 minutes

Turkey Salsa Rolls

INGREDIENTS

¼ cup	packaged salsa
1 tablespoon	cilantro chopped
1 tablespoon	minced purple onion
2	large tomato wraps
4 ounces	turkey sliced
4 ounces	Monterey Jack cheese with jalapeno peppers shredded

DIRECTIONS

1. In a small bowl, combine the salsa, onion and cilantro; set aside.

2. Place the tomato wraps on a cutting board and spread salsa down the center of the wrap. Top each wrap with turkey and cheese. Fold in sides and roll-up.

3. Place the wraps end side down and grill for 3 minutes or until wraps are golden and cheese is melted.

4. Cut in quarters and serve warm.

Chicken Tenders with Marinade

INGREDIENTS

16 chicken tenders
(about 2 ½ pounds)

marinade

DIRECTIONS

1. Prepare your choice of marinade from the selections to follow your own recipe.

2. When finished, add chicken tenders and mix with marinade to coat. Allow to stand 10 minutes to blend flavors.

3. Remove chicken from marinade and discard. Place chicken tenders on preheated grill and cook for 4 minutes or until a meat thermometer inserted into center registers 180°F.

FIERY FRUIT MARINADE

INGREDIENTS

½ cup fresh lime juice

¼ cup fresh orange juice

¼ cup prepared hot salsa

¼ cup fresh or canned papaya juice

1 tablespoon canola oil

2 tablespoons fresh cilantro
chopped

1 teaspoon ground cumin

1 teaspoon salt

DIRECTIONS

1. Mix all the ingredients in a medium bowl.

Tip from the Playbook

Surprise your game day guests with a spin on this traditional crowd pleaser. We have selected 3 flavorful marinades that appeal to a variety of taste buds. Try serving all 3 at your next party and win everyone over.

WESTERN SMOKEY BBQ SAUCE

INGREDIENTS

1	**small yellow onion** chopped
¼ cup	**dark brown sugar**
3	**large garlic cloves** chopped
2 teaspoons	**celery seed**
2 teaspoons	**dry mustard**
1 cup	**tomato sauce**
¼ cup	**cider vinegar**
¼ cup	**low sodium soy sauce**
¼ cup	**Worcestershire sauce**
1 teaspoon	**bottle liquid smoke**

DIRECTIONS

1. Combine all ingredients in a small saucepan and bring to a boil, stirring.
2. Reduce heat and simmer 8 minutes or until slightly thickened, stirring occasionally.
3. Cool the sauce before mixing with the tenders.

HONEY MUSTARD MARINADE

INGREDIENTS

2 tablespoons	**honey**
3 tablespoons	**Dijon mustard**
2 tablespoons	**fresh lemon juice**
1 tablespoon	**extra-virgin olive oil**
1 teaspoon	**lemon pepper**

DIRECTIONS

1. Soften the honey in a microwave oven for 15 seconds.
2. Combine all of the ingredients and mix thoroughly into a thick paste.

Thai Chicken Skewers with Peanut Sauce

INGREDIENTS

8	**8-inch wooden skewers**
2 tablespoons	**fresh cilantro** minced
2	**large garlic cloves** minced
1 teaspoon	**fresh ginger** grated
¼ cup	**low sodium soy sauce**
2 tablespoons	**fresh lime juice**
4	**chicken breasts** boneless and skinless
2 tablespoons	**fresh cilantro** chopped

DIRECTIONS

1. Soak wooden skewers in water in a 9-inch pie plate for at least 20 minutes.

2. In a resealable plastic bag, combine the cilantro, garlic, ginger, soy sauce and lime juice.

3. Cut the chicken into 1-inch cubes and add to the marinade. Seal bag and shake to coat the chicken. Refrigerate 2 hours or overnight.

4. Remove chicken from marinade and discard marinade. Thread the chicken onto the skewers.

5. Place the skewers on the preheated grill horizontally and cook for 4 minutes or until a meat thermometer inserted into center of the chicken registers 180°F.

6. Arrange the chicken skewers on a platter, sprinkle with chopped cilantro.

7. Serve with Thai Peanut Sauce (recipe to follow).

SEE PHOTO on page 17

THAI PEANUT SAUCE

INGREDIENTS

6 tablespoons	chunky peanut butter
3 tablespoons	honey
3 tablespoons	low sodium soy sauce
2 tablespoons	fresh lime juice
1 teaspoon	Asian garlic chile sauce
1 tablespoon	fresh ginger grated

DIRECTIONS

1. In a small bowl, combine all of the ingredients and let stand to blend flavors.

2. Serve with Thai Chicken Skewers (recipe on previous page).

Chicken Asiago Wrap

INGREDIENTS

3 tablespoon	sundried tomato vinaigrette
2 tablespoon	black olives chopped
1 tablespoon	Italian parsley chopped
2	large whole wheat wraps
4 ounces	Sausalito flavored chicken thinly sliced
4 ounces	Asiago cheese thinly sliced
1	medium tomato sliced
½ cup	spinach leaves
2 tablespoon	extra virgin olive oil

DIRECTIONS

1. In a small bowl, combine vinaigrette, olives and parsley; set aside.

2. Place wheat wraps on a cutting board and spread the olive mixture in center of the wheat wrap. Top each wheat wrap with chicken, cheese, tomato and spinach. Tuck in the sides and roll-up.

3. Place the wrap seam side down on the grill and cook about 4 minutes or until tortilla is lightly browned.

4. Cut into quarters and serve.

Plates needed: Grilling Plates
Preheat temperature: Medium
Estimated cooking time: 5 minutes

Grilled Wonton

INGREDIENTS

2	**chicken breast halves** boneless, skinless
½ cup	**bean sprouts** finely chopped
¼ cup	**water chestnuts** finely diced
1	**garlic clove** finely minced
¼ cup	**hoisin sauce**
2 tablespoons	**low sodium soy sauce**
1 tablespoon	**Szechuan chili sauce**
16	**wonton square wrappers**

DIRECTIONS

1. Place the chicken on the preheated grill and cook for 5 minutes or until meat thermometer inserted into center registers 180°F.

2. Place the chicken on a cutting board. Cool and chop into very small pieces.

3. Place the chicken, bean sprouts, water chestnuts, garlic, hoisin sauce, soy sauce, and chili sauce into a large bowl. Mix well.

4. Place 1 wonton square on a flat surface. Spoon 1 heaping tablespoon of the chicken and vegetable mixture onto one-half of the square.

5. Brush water on the edges of the wonton wrapper. Fold in half, creating a triangle, and press the edges to seal.

6. Repeat with the remaining wonton wrappers.

7. Place 8 wontons on the preheated grill and cook for 5 minutes or until browned and cooked through. Repeat until all are cooked.

8. Serve with additional soy sauce, if desired.

APPETIZERS

Plates needed: Top Grilling Plate; Bottom Bake Plate
Preheat temperature: High
Estimated cooking time: 7-9 minutes

Stuffed Chile Rellenos

INGREDIENTS

1 cup	**Monterey Jack cheese** grated
1 cup	**brown rice** cooked
½	**small white onion** minced
¼ cup	**pine nuts** toasted
¼ cup	**fresh cilantro** minced
¼ cup	**currants**
½ teaspoon	**red chili powder**
½ teaspoon	**salt**
¼ teaspoon	**ground cumin**
¼ teaspoon	**ground nutmeg**
4	**fresh or canned poblano chiles** peeled, seeds and stem removed
2	**eggs** slightly beaten
1 cup	**unsifted all-purpose flour**
¼ cup	**yellow corn meal**
2 tablespoons	**canola oil**

DIRECTIONS

1. In a medium bowl, combine the first 10 ingredients and mix well.

2. Cut a short vertical slit in each chile and stuff with ¼ of the rice mixture. Secure the slit closed.

3. Place the eggs in a pie plate or shallow glass dish. Combine the flour and corn meal in another pie plate or shallow glass dish. Dip the chiles in the egg, then coat in the flour.

4. Remove all excess flour from the mixture.

5. Drizzle 1-tablespoon of oil into the preheated baking plate. Place the chiles in the baking plate and drizzle with the remaining oil.

6. Cook for 7 minutes or until the cheese is melted and the chiles are golden brown.

7. Garnish with salsa, sour cream or guacamole, if desired.

POINTS

Plates needed: Grilling Plates
Preheat temperature: High
Estimated cooking time: 3 minutes

SEE PHOTO on page 18

All-American Beef &
Blue Cheese Sliders

INGREDIENTS

¼ cup	crumbled blue cheese
2 tablespoons	green onion minced
1 teaspoon	salt
½ teaspoon	black pepper
1 teaspoon	extra-virgin olive oil
1 pound	extra-lean ground beef 7% fat
8	small leaves of curly-leaf green lettuce
8	slider buns or dinner rolls split

DIRECTIONS

1. In a large bowl, mix together the blue cheese, onion, salt, pepper and oil. Add ground beef and lightly mix; do not over mix.

2. Divide the ground beef mixture into 8 equal portions and form into ½–inch thick patties.

3. Place the patties on a preheated grill and cook for 3 minutes, or until desired doneness.

4. Assemble each slider by placing 1 leaf of lettuce on the bottom half of each roll. Place a cooked beef patty onto the lettuce. Top each patty with the remaining half of the roll.

Hot Sausage Sandwiches

INGREDIENTS

1 large	**garlic clove** finely minced
1 teaspoon	**dried Italian seasoning**
¼ teaspoon	**black pepper** coarsely ground
1 pound	**low-fat hot Italian sausage links**
1	**tomato** sliced
1	**green pepper** seeded and thinly sliced
1	**small purple onion** thinly sliced
¼ cup	**non-fat mayonnaise**
4	**sandwich buns** split and toasted

DIRECTIONS

1. In a small bowl, combine the garlic, Italian seasoning and pepper; sprinkle the mixture over sausages and vegetables.

2. Arrange the sausages horizontally on a preheated grill and place the tomato, green pepper and onion around the links.

3. Grill for 6 minutes, or until a meat thermometer inserted into center of the sausage registers 160°F.

4. Spread mayonnaise on the bottom of each bun and add the sausage and vegetable mixture. Top with remaining half of bun.

Plates needed: Grilling Plates
Preheat temperature: Medium
Estimated cooking time: 15 minutes

Eggplant Parmesan Focaccia

INGREDIENTS

1	small eggplant
1 teaspoon	salt
½ teaspoon	black pepper coarsely ground
3 tablespoons	extra-virgin olive oil
4 large	fresh basil leaves minced *(substitute ¼ teaspoon dried basil)*
1 large	rosemary focaccia bread split horizontally
¼ cup	prepared marinara sauce
6 slices	non-fat mozzarella cheese
¼ cup	parmesan cheese grated

DIRECTIONS

1. Peel the eggplant and cut into ¼-inch slices.

2. Arrange the slices on a double-thickness of paper towels. Sprinkle with salt and let stand for 20 minutes. Rinse the eggplant and pat dry.

3. Lightly brush each slice with 2-tablespoons oil and season with pepper and basil.

4. Place half of the eggplant slices on a preheated grill and cook for 8 minutes or until tender. Remove from the grill and keep warm. Repeat with remaining slices.

5. Spread marinara on the bottom of half a loaf of focaccia bread. Top with slices of eggplant and mozzarella and parmesan cheese. Cover with remaining half of focaccia loaf. Brush outside of bread with remaining 1-tablespoon of oil. Place on preheated grill and cook for 4 minutes, until the cheese is melted.

6. Brush outside of bread with remaining 1-tablespoon of oil. Place on preheated grill and cook for 4 minutes or until the cheese is melted.

APPETIZERS

Plates needed: Grilling Plates & Bottom Bake Plate
Preheat temperature: Medium High
Estimated cooking time: 10 minutes

servings **4**

Quesadillas Rapidas

INGREDIENTS

1 ½ cups	**pepper strips**
1	**medium onion** thinly sliced
2	**large garlic cloves** minced
½ pound	**grilled pork loin** cut in strips
2 tablespoons	**cilantro** chopped
½ teaspoon	**cumin** ground
½ teaspoon	**oregano**
½ teaspoon	**coarse salt**
¼ teaspoon	**black pepper** coarsely ground
1 cup	**Cheddar Jack cheese blend** shredded
4	**10-inch large tortillas**

DIRECTIONS

1. Cook peppers, onion and garlic in a preheated baking plate for 3 minutes or until the onion is softened. Remove and combine with pork, cilantro, and seasonings in a medium bowl; toss to mix.

2. Cool the baking plate and replace with the bottom grill plate.

3. Place 1 tortilla on the work surface and add ½ of the pork mixture. Top with ½ of the cheese and cover with 1 tortilla.

4. Carefully place on preheated grill and cook for 3 minutes or until cheese is melted and tortillas are lightly browned.

5. Remove to a serving plate and repeat with the remaining tortillas, pork mixture and cheese.

6. Garnish with sour cream, salsa, and chopped cilantro, if desired.

Asian Noodle Steak Salad

INGREDIENTS

½ pound	**lean beef steak**
	well trimmed
8 ounces	**vermicelli pasta**
	cooked and drained
1	**red pepper**
	seeded and thinly sliced
1 cup	**fresh bean sprouts**
¼ cup	**low sodium soy sauce**
½ teaspoon	**Asian chili oil**
1 teaspoon	**brown sugar**
1 medium	**garlic clove**
	minced
½ teaspoon	**ground ginger**
¼ teaspoon	**black pepper**
¼ cup	**dry roasted peanuts**
	coarsely chopped

DIRECTIONS

1. Cut the beef into very thin slices.
2. Grill the beef on a preheated grill for 3 minutes or to desired doneness.
3. In a large serving bowl, mix the beef with the pasta, red pepper and bean sprouts.
4. In a small bowl, prepare the salad dressing by combining the soy sauce, chili oil, brown sugar, garlic, ginger and pepper.
5. Pour the dressing over the salad and toss until well mixed.
6. Top with the chopped peanuts.

APPETIZERS

Grilled and Chilled Seafood Salad

INGREDIENTS

12 medium	sea scallops
8 ounces	halibut cut into 1-inch pieces
12 small	shrimp with tails removed, cleaned and deveined
3 tablespoons	fresh lemon juice
½ teaspoons	black pepper
1	yellow bell pepper thinly sliced
1	green bell pepper thinly sliced
1	red bell pepper thinly sliced
3 tablespoons	fresh parsley minced
¼ cup	extra-virgin olive oil
2 tablespoons	tarragon vinegar
½ teaspoon	salt

DIRECTIONS

1. In a medium bowl, mix the seafood with 1 tablespoon of lemon juice and ¼-teaspoon of black pepper.

2. Place the scallops and halibut on the preheated grilling plate and cook for 4 minutes or until scallops register 145°F on the meat thermometer.

3. Remove the scallops and add the shrimp with the halibut.

4. Cook for an additional 2 minutes or until the shrimp is pink and cooked through and halibut registers 145°F on the meat thermometer.

5. Cool the seafood.

6. In a large bowl, mix the sliced peppers, parsley and cooled seafood.

7. In a small bowl, whisk together the oil, vinegar, remaining 2 tablespoons of lemon juice, salt and remaining ¼-teaspoon of pepper until well-blended.

8. Pour over the seafood and mix lightly. Refrigerate at least 1 hour before serving.

POINTS

Plates needed: Top Grilling Plate; Bottom Bake Plate
Preheat temperature: High
Estimated cooking time: 20 minutes

Easy Focaccia

INGREDIENTS

1	**8-ounce package refrigerated garlic breadsticks**
½ cup	**Asiago cheese** shredded
½ cup	**parsley** chopped
2 tablespoons	**fresh rosemary** chopped
1 tablespoon	**olive oil**

DIRECTIONS

1. Unroll breadsticks (do not separate) and lay out on a preheated grill.

2. Sprinkle evenly with cheese. Top with parsley and rosemary. Drizzle oil over all.

3. Bake for 20 minutes or until crust is golden and cheese is melted.

4. Using pot holders, remove baking plate from grill and place on heat resistant surface. Use a nylon spatula to remove the breadsticks from the baking plate. Serve warm.

APPETIZERS

NEW ORLEANS
PORK RIBS
page 45

BEEF TENDERLOIN CHURRASCO
with CHIMICHURRI SAUCE
page 47

PIAZZA CHICKEN &
SPINACH   page 55

ITALIANO BEEF &
MOZZARELLA BURGERS page 65

New Orleans Pork Ribs

INGREDIENTS

1 ½ pound	boneless country-style pork ribs well trimmed
¼ cup	tomato paste
¼ cup	cider vinegar
2 tablespoons	honey
2 tablespoons	water
1 tablespoon	extra virgin olive oil
2 teaspoons	dry mustard
½ teaspoon	Tabasco sauce
1	garlic clove minced
¼ cup	chopped onion

DIRECTIONS

1. Score the ribs with a knife to prevent the meat from curling as it grills.
2. In a small saucepan, mix the remaining ingredients and cook for about 5 minutes or until thickened; keep warm.
3. Place ribs on a preheated grill and cook 4 minutes.
4. Open the grill and baste the ribs with sauce.
5. Grill another 4 minutes or until meat registers 160°F on a meat thermometer.
6. Serve with the remaining warm sauce.

See photo on page 41

Tip from the Playbook

Hit a Grand Slam with ENTREES

Plates needed: Grilling Plates
Preheat temperature: Medium
Estimated cooking time: 8 minutes

Citrus Pork Panini with Chipotle Mayonnaise

INGREDIENTS

2 tablespoons	fresh lime juice
2 tablespoons	fresh orange juice
2 teaspoons	ground cumin
12 ounces	pork tenderloin *well trimmed*
2	jalapeño rolls or soft French rolls
4 tablespoons	Chipotle Mayonnaise
1 teaspoon	extra-virgin olive oil
1 cup	green cabbage *shredded*
½	small red onion *thinly sliced*
1	ripe tomato *chopped*

DIRECTIONS

1. In a resealable plastic bag, mix the juices and the cumin. Slice the pork into ½-inch thick slices and place in the plastic bag. Seal tightly and turn the bag several times to coat the pork with the marinade.

2. Refrigerate for 1 to 4 hours. Discard the marinade.

3. Place the pork slices on the preheated grilling plate and cook for 4 minutes or until meat registers 160°F on meat thermometer.

4. Split the French rolls in half horizontally. Spread each cut side with 1 tablespoon of Chipotle Mayonnaise. Divide the pork between the 2 bottom roll halves and top with the remaining roll halves. Lightly brush the top of the rolls with oil.

5. Place the panini on the grilling plate and cook for 2 to 3 minutes, or until the bread is golden brown.

6. To serve, carefully open panini and stuff with cabbage, onion and tomatoes.

Plates needed: Grilling Plates
Preheat temperature: High
Estimated cooking time: 3 minutes

servings **4**

Beef Tenderloin Churrasco with Chimichurri Sauce

INGREDIENTS

1 cup	fresh flat leaf parsley leaves
8	medium garlic cloves coarsely chopped
1	medium jalapeño pepper coarsely chopped
1 teaspoon	dried oregano
½ teaspoon	salt
½ cup	extra-virgin olive oil
¼ cup	red wine vinegar
4	6-ounce boneless beef tenderloin steaks fat removed

DIRECTIONS

1. In a blender, combine the parsley, garlic, pepper, oregano, salt, oil and vinegar; blend until smooth.

2. Place the steaks in a large plastic bag and add half of the sauce mixture. Reserve the remaining sauce.

3. Seal the bag and squeeze between your fingers to evenly coat the steaks.

4. Refrigerate for at least one hour or overnight.

5. Remove the steaks from the marinade.

6. Place the steaks on the preheated grill and discard marinade.

7. Grill for about 3 minutes or until the meat registers at 145°F for medium rare or 160°F for medium on a meat thermometer.

8. Slice thinly across the grain and fan onto serving plate.

9. Spoon reserved Chimichurri sauce over steaks and serve.

47
POINTS

See photo on page 42

Plates needed: Grilling Plates
Preheat temperature: High
Estimated cooking time: 12 minutes

Tenderloin Steaks with Grilled Mushrooms & Blue Cheese

INGREDIENTS

4 ounces	**fresh mushrooms** sliced
1	**strip turkey bacon** cut into 4 pieces
4	**beef tenderloin steaks** well trimmed, 4 ounces each
½ teaspoon	**salt**
¼ teaspoon	**coarsely ground pepper**
4 teaspoons	**crumbled blue or gorgonzola cheese**

DIRECTIONS

1. Place the mushrooms on the preheated grill plate and top with the bacon. Cook for 4 minutes or until bacon is crisp and mushrooms are browned around the edges.

2. Remove bacon and reserve for another use. Set aside the mushrooms and keep warm.

3. Season steaks with salt and pepper. Place steaks on preheated grill plates and cook for 4 minutes or until meat registers 145°F for medium rare or 160°F for medium on a meat thermometer.

4. To serve, top each steak with 1-teaspoon of the crumbled cheese and grilled mushrooms.

Plates needed: Grilling Plates
Preheat temperature: High
Estimated cooking time: 4 minutes

servings **4**

Entertaining Beef Tenderloin

INGREDIENTS

½ cup   fresh flat leaf parsley leaves

2   large garlic cloves
coarsely chopped

1 tablespoon   fresh thyme leaves

½ teaspoon   salt

¼ teaspoon   coarse ground black pepper

4   boneless beef tenderloin steaks
fat removed
about 6 ounces each

½ cup   plain yogurt

DIRECTIONS

1. In small bowl, combine the parsley, garlic, thyme, salt and pepper. Rub half of the mixture over the steaks.

2. Place the steaks on the preheated grill plates and cook for 4 minutes or until the meat registers 145°F for medium rare or 160°F for medium on a meat thermometer.

3. Blend the remaining herb mixture into the yogurt and drizzle it over the steaks just before serving.

POINTS

Plates needed: Grilling Plates
Preheat temperature: High
Estimated cooking time: 4 minutes

Steak Tacos with Avocado Salsa

INGREDIENTS

1 **medium avocado**
peeled and chopped

¾ cup **canned black beans**
rinsed and drained

1 **medium yellow tomato**
chopped *

¼ cup **purple onion**
minced

2 tablespoons **cilantro**
minced

2 **serrano peppers**
finely chopped

2 **large garlic cloves**
minced

½ teaspoon **salt**

juice of 1 lime
about 3 tablespoons

1 tablespoon **taco seasoning**

1 teaspoon **Montreal steak
seasoning**

2 pounds **skirt steak**

**soft flour or crisp corn
taco shells**

romaine lettuce
shredded

DIRECTIONS

1. In medium bowl, combine the first 9 ingredients. Toss to coat the avocado with lime juice. Set aside for the flavors to blend.

2. In small bowl, combine the taco seasoning and steak seasoning. Use to season the steak on both sides.

3. Place the steak on the preheated grill. Cook 3 minutes for medium rare or 5 minutes for medium or until the meat registers 145°F for medium rare or 160°F for medium on a meat thermometer.

4. Remove from the grill and onto a plate or cutting board. Cover with foil and let stand at least 6 minutes. Thinly slice.

5. To assemble tacos, place some lettuce on a taco shell and top with beef slices and avocado salsa.

   * *Ripe red tomatoes can be substituted for yellow tomatoes, if they are not available.*

ENTREES

Simple Lemon Thyme Turkey

INGREDIENTS

1 pound	turkey breast boneless, skinless
¼ cup	extra-virgin olive oil
¼ cup	fresh lemon juice
1 tablespoon	lemon zest
2	medium garlic cloves finely minced
4 tablespoons	fresh thyme finely minced
1 teaspoon	salt
¼ teaspoon	black pepper

DIRECTIONS

1. Slice the turkey breast horizontally across the grain into 1-inch thick slices and place in a shallow glass baking dish or pie plate.

2. In a small bowl, whisk together the remaining ingredients. Pour the marinade over the turkey, turning a few times to coat.

3. Cover tightly with plastic wrap and refrigerate for 1 to 4 hours, turning once. Remove the meat from the marinade and discard.

4. Place the turkey slices on the preheated grill plate and cook for 5 minutes or until the turkey registers 180°F on a meat thermometer.

POINTS

Chicken Piccata

INGREDIENTS

4	**6-ounce chicken breasts** boneless, skinless
¼ cup	**all-purpose flour**
1 teaspoon	**salt**
½ teaspoon	**lemon pepper**
3 tablespoons	**extra-virgin olive oil**
3 tablespoons	**low-fat margarine**
3 tablespoons	**fresh flat leaf parsley** minced
3 tablespoons	**capers**
¼ cup	**chicken broth**
3 tablespoons	**fresh lemon juice**
1	**lemon** cut in wedges

DIRECTIONS

1. Place the chicken breasts between two pieces of waxed paper or plastic wrap and pound to a thickness of ½-inch.

2. In a shallow glass baking dish or pie plate, combine the flour, salt and lemon pepper and press each chicken breast into the flour mixture, turning to coat all sides.

3. Pour 1-tablespoon of oil in the preheated baking plate. Shake the excess flour from the chicken and place the chicken in the baking plate. Drizzle the chicken with 1-tablespoon of oil and cook for 4 minutes or until chicken registers 180°F on a meat thermometer.

4. In a small saucepan, melt margarine with remaining 1-tablespoon olive oil and add the parsley, capers, chicken broth and lemon juice. Bring to boil; lower heat and simmer for 3 minutes.

5. Serve the chicken garnished with sauce and lemon wedges.

ENTRÉES

Artichoke Stuffed Chicken

INGREDIENTS

14 ounce	canned artichoke hearts packed in water, drained
2 tablespoons	fresh lemon juice
1 teaspoon	lemon zest
2 tablespoons	Romano cheese grated
1	large garlic clove chopped
2 tablespoons	extra-virgin olive oil
4	chicken breasts boneless, skinless about 5 ounces each
1 teaspoon	salt
¼ teaspoon	black pepper

DIRECTIONS

1. Place the artichoke hearts, lemon juice, lemon zest, cheese, garlic and olive oil in a food processor and process until blended.

2. Place the chicken on a clean cutting surface. With the tip of a sharp knife, slit each breast horizontally without cutting all the way through to create a pocket.

3. Stuff ¼ of the stuffing into each chicken breast and press the edges to close. Fasten opening with toothpicks.

4. Season the chicken with salt and pepper.

5. Place the chicken breasts on the preheated grill. Cook for 6 minutes or until chicken registers 180°F on meat thermometer.

6. Remove toothpicks before serving.

POINTS

Caribbean Jerk Chicken with Saffron Rice

INGREDIENTS

1 tablespoon	**fresh parsley** minced
1 teaspoon	**ground paprika**
½ cup	**fresh lemon juice**
2 tablespoons	**Szechuan chili sauce**
2 tablespoons	**oil**
1 tablespoon	**yellow mustard**
4	**chicken breasts** boneless, skinless about 4 ounces each
1 cup	**long grain white rice**
¼ cup	**onion** chopped
¼ teaspoon	**saffron threads** crumbled
½ teaspoon	**salt**
¼ teaspoon	**white pepper**
2 cups	**low-sodium, reduced-fat chicken broth**

DIRECTIONS

1. Combine parsley, paprika, lemon juice, chili sauce, oil and mustard in a 1-quart plastic bag. Seal bag and squeeze between your fingers to blend ingredients. Add chicken and reseal the bag. Shake to coat the chicken with marinade.

2. Refrigerate for at least 1 hour.

3. In a medium saucepan, mix rice, onion, saffron, salt, pepper, and chicken broth; bring to boil. Reduce heat to low; cover and simmer for 25 minutes or until rice is tender and liquid is absorbed.

4. Remove chicken from marinade. Place chicken on the grill and discard marinade. Grill for 7 minutes or until the chicken registers 170°F on a meat thermometer.

5. Serve with cooked rice.

Plates needed: Grilling Plates; Bottom Bake Plate
Preheat temperature: Medium High
Estimated cooking time: 9 minutes

servings **4**

Piazza Chicken & Spinach

INGREDIENTS

1	**small red pepper** seeded and chopped
1 cup	**loosely packed fresh spinach without stems** chopped
¼ cup	**onion** chopped
1 tablespoon	**fresh basil** chopped
1 teaspoon	**salt**
½ teaspoon	**pepper**
1 tablespoon	**extra-virgin olive oil**
6	**4-ounce chicken breast halves** boneless and skinless
6	**1-ounce slices low-fat mozzarella cheese**

DIRECTIONS

1. On preheated baking plate, cook red pepper and onion for about 3 minutes, until the onion is softened. Add spinach and cook until the spinach is softened. Transfer vegetable mixture to a medium bowl. Add basil, salt, pepper and oil; toss lightly.

2. Place the chicken on a clean cutting surface. With the tip of a sharp knife, slit each breast horizontally without cutting all the way through to create a pocket.

3. Place one slice of cheese inside each pocket and spoon spinach stuffing over the cheese slices.

4. Close each pocket by pressing the edges of the chicken together lightly. If desired, fasten with a toothpick.

5. Allow grill to cool and carefully replace baking plate with the bottom grill plate. Preheat grill and add chicken breasts. Cook for 6 minutes or until the chicken is done and registers 180°F on a meat thermometer.

6. Remove toothpicks before serving.

SEE PHOTO page 43

Grilled Halibut with Citrus-Caper Sauce

INGREDIENTS

2 tablespoons	low-fat margarine
2 tablespoons	extra-virgin olive oil
¼ cup	fresh lemon juice
¼ cup	fresh orange juice
2 tablespoons	capers drained
¼ teaspoon	Dijon mustard
4	halibut steaks about 6 ounces each
1 teaspoon	lemon pepper
1 tablespoons	fresh Italian parsley chopped

DIRECTIONS

1. In a small saucepan, melt the margarine with the oil over low heat. Add the lemon, orange juice, capers and mustard. While stirring, bring to a boil, then reduce heat and simmer 2 to 3 minutes.

2. Season fish with lemon pepper and place the steaks on the preheated grill plate.

3. Cook for 7 minutes. Check and continue grilling if necessary.

4. To serve, top each steak with sauce and parsley.

ENTRÉES

Hot & Sweet Thai Shrimp with Fresh Papaya

INGREDIENTS

2	**medium garlic cloves** minced
¼ teaspoon	**dried red pepper flakes**
2 tablespoons	**Thai fish sauce**
1 tablespoon	**lime juice**
1 tablespoon	**orange juice**
2 teaspoons	**honey**
1 teaspoon	**peanut oil**
1 pound	**jumbo shrimp** peeled and deveined, tails on
1	**ripe papaya** peeled, seeded and sliced
1 tablespoon	**fresh mint** chopped
1 tablespoon	**green onion** minced

DIRECTIONS

1. Place the first 7 ingredients in a 1-quart plastic bag. Seal bag and squeeze between your fingers to blend ingredients. Add shrimp and reseal the bag. Shake to coat shrimp with marinade.

2. Refrigerate for 1 hour.

3. Remove shrimp from the marinade and discard marinade.

4. Grill shrimp for 3 minutes or until it is pink and cooked through.

5. Serve shrimp on a bed of papaya. Garnish with green onion and mint.

POINTS

Spinach Stuffed Eggplant

INGREDIENTS

2	medium eggplants
½ teaspoon	salt
5 ounces	frozen chopped spinach thawed and well drained
½ cup	low-fat feta cheese crumbled
½ cup	non-fat ricotta cheese
2	large garlic cloves crushed
1 teaspoon	dried oregano
½ teaspoon	nutmeg
1 teaspoon	salt
¼ teaspoon	black pepper
1 teaspoon	balsamic vinegar
1 tablespoon	extra-virgin olive oil
10 ounces	spaghetti cooked
1 cup	prepared marinara sauce heated
½ cup	Romano cheese grated

DIRECTIONS

1. Slice eggplant lengthwise into 1½-inch thick slices.

2. Arrange on a double-thickness of paper towels and sprinkle with salt. Let stand for 10 minutes.

3. Rinse the eggplant and pat dry.

4. With the tip of a sharp knife, cut a slit in each eggplant horizontally, without cutting all the way through, to create a large pocket.

5. In a medium bowl, thoroughly mix the spinach, feta, ricotta cheese, garlic, oregano, nutmeg, salt, pepper and vinegar. Stuff each eggplant with the spinach stuffing and press the edges together to close the pocket. Fasten opening with toothpicks.

6. Brush the eggplant lightly with oil and season with additional salt and pepper. Place several eggplant slices on the preheated grill plate in a single layer and close the lid.

7. Cook for 9 minutes or until eggplant is tender. Remove from grill and keep warm. Repeat with remaining eggplant.

8. Serve on a bed of pasta topped with sauce. Garnish with Romano cheese.

Grown-Up Grilled Cheese

INGREDIENTS

4	slices hearty wheat bread
2 tablespoons	melted butter
1	large tomato sliced
6	slices crisp bacon
4	slices white Cheddar cheese about ⅓ pound
½ cup	arugula
2 tablespoons	bottled balsamic vinaigrette

DIRECTIONS

1. Spread melted butter on one side of each slice of bread.

2. Place 2 slices of bread buttered side down on cutting board. Top each slice of bread with tomato, bacon, cheese and arugula. Drizzle each sandwich with 1 tablespoon vinaigrette. Cover with remaining slices of bread with buttered side up.

3. Place on preheated grill and cook for 3 minutes or until sandwich is golden and cheese is melted.

Plates needed: Top Grilling Plate; Bottom Bake Plate
Preheat temperature: High
Estimated cooking time: 20-24 minutes

Deep Dish Pizza

INGREDIENTS

1 package	**refrigerated classic pizza crust** 13.8 ounces
1 cup	**bottled or prepared marinara sauce**
2 cups	**Mozzarella cheese** shredded
½ cup	**Parmesan & Romano cheese** shredded
½ cup	**pepperoni** sliced

DIRECTIONS

1. Remove pizza crust from package and press into bottom and sides of the baking plate.

2. Spread marinara sauce on bottom crust. Top with cheeses and pepperoni. Place plate into bottom of grill.

3. Preheat the grill.

4. Close the grill cover and bake for 20 minutes or until crust is golden and cheese is melted and browned.

5. Using pot holders, remove plate from grill and place on trivet or cooling rack. Use nylon spatula to remove pizza from plate.

Favorite Beef Burgers

INGREDIENTS

1 pound	lean ground beef
½ teaspoon	garlic powder
½ teaspoon	salt
¼ teaspoon	black pepper
4	seeded hamburger buns
	split and toasted
4	leaves curly green leaf lettuce
4	slices ripe tomato

DIRECTIONS

1. Divide ground beef mixture into 4 equal portions. Lightly flatten each to form a ½-inch thick burger. Season with garlic powder, salt and pepper.

2. Place burgers on the preheated grill and cook for 4 minutes, or until desired doneness.

3. Serve on buns with lettuce, tomatoes, and other condiments of your choice.

Plates needed: Grilling Plates
Preheat temperature: High
Estimated cooking time: 4 minutes

Barbequed Cowboy Burgers

INGREDIENTS

½ cup   tomato sauce

2 tablespoons   finely chopped onion

1   medium garlic clove
minced

2 tablespoons   Worcestershire sauce

1 tablespoon   prepared yellow mustard

1 tablespoon   brown sugar

1 pound   extra lean ground round

4   whole grain
hamburger buns
split and toasted

DIRECTIONS

1. In a small saucepan, combine tomato sauce, onion, garlic, Worcestershire sauce, mustard and brown sugar. Bring to boil, stirring; reduce heat and simmer for 10 minutes and cool completely.

2. In a large bowl, mix the beef with the barbeque sauce.

3. Shape into 4 patties and refrigerate at least 1 hour.

4. Place the burgers on the preheated grill and cook for 4 minutes or to desired doneness.

5. Serve on buns with lettuce, tomatoes, dill pickles and other condiments of your choice.

Plates needed: Grilling Plates
Preheat temperature: High
Estimated cooking time: 4 minutes

servings **4**

Cheesy Beef Burgers

INGREDIENTS

1 pound	lean ground chuck
1 cup	low-fat cheddar cheese shredded
1 tablespoon	green onion chopped
1 teaspoon	salt
½ teaspoon	garlic powder
½ teaspoon	black pepper
1 tablespoon	Worcestershire sauce
4	sourdough hamburger buns split and toasted

DIRECTIONS

1. In a large bowl, combine beef, cheese, onion, salt, garlic powder, pepper and Worcestershire sauce; shape into 4 hamburger patties.

2. Place the burgers on the preheated grill and cook for 4 minutes or to desired doneness.

3. To serve, place each burger on a sourdough bun and top with condiments of your choice.

Plates needed: Grilling Plates
Preheat temperature: High
Estimated cooking time: 4 minutes

Ranchero Burgers

INGREDIENTS

¾ pound	**extra lean ground round**
½ cup	**canned kidney beans** drained and mashed
2	**large garlic cloves** minced
¼ cup	**prepared barbeque sauce**
½ teaspoon	**salt**
½ teaspoon	**black pepper**
4	**sesame-seeded hamburger buns** split and toasted

DIRECTIONS

1. In a large bowl, combine beef, beans, garlic, barbeque sauce, salt and pepper; shape into 4 patties.

2. Place the burgers on the preheated grill and cook for 4 minutes or to desired doneness.

3. Place each hamburger on a sesame bun and serve with your choice of condiments.

Italiano Beef & Mozzarella Burgers

INGREDIENTS

1 pound	lean ground chuck
1 teaspoon	dried Italian seasoning
1 teaspoon	ground oregano
1	egg white
1	medium garlic clove minced
¼ cup	low-fat Italian salad dressing
4	slices Ciabatta bread ½-inch thick, lightly toasted
4	lettuce leaves
1	ripe tomato thinly sliced
4	slices part-skim Mozzarella cheese
½	purple onion thinly sliced

DIRECTIONS

1. In a large bowl, combine beef, Italian seasoning, oregano, egg white and garlic; shape into 4 patties.

2. Place the burgers on the preheated grill and cook for 4 minutes or to desired doneness.

3. Drizzle the Italian salad dressing on the Ciabatta bread and top each with the lettuce, tomato, cheese and onion.

4. Place the cooked hamburger patties on top and serve.

See Photo on page 44

POINTS

Plates needed: Grilling Plates
Preheat temperature: High
Estimated cooking time: 4 minutes

Portabella Mushroom Burgers

INGREDIENTS

4	**Portabella mushrooms** cleaned and stems removed
2 tablespoons	**extra virgin olive oil**
2 tablespoons	**balsamic vinegar**
2	**large garlic cloves** minced
1 tablespoon	**dried Italian seasoning**
1 teaspoon	**coarsely ground black pepper**
4	**Kaiser or crusty sandwich rolls** split

DIRECTIONS

1. Drizzle the oil and vinegar over each mushroom and sprinkle with the garlic, Italian seasoning and pepper.

2. Place the mushrooms on the preheated grill, underside facing up and cook for 5 minutes or until mushrooms are tender and lightly browned on edges.

3. Serve on Kaiser rolls with condiments such as sliced onion, low-fat Mozzarella cheese or sundried tomatoes.

ENTRÉES

Swiss Turkey Burgers

INGREDIENTS

1 pound	lean ground turkey
6 ounces	low-fat Swiss cheese shredded
1	egg white
1 tablespoon	Dijon mustard
¼ cup	fresh bread crumbs
1 teaspoon	seasoned salt
1 teaspoon	black pepper
4	onion rolls split and toasted

DIRECTIONS

1. In a large bowl, combine turkey, Swiss cheese, egg white, mustard, bread crumbs, salt and pepper; shape into 4 patties.

2. Place the burgers in the preheated grill and cook for 6 minutes or until meat thermometer inserted into center registers 170°F.

3. Place each burger in a roll and serve with condiments of your choice.

Plates needed: Grilling Plates
Preheat temperature: High
Estimated cooking time: 6 minutes

Ranch Style Chicken Burgers

INGREDIENTS

1 pound	lean ground chicken
2 tablespoons	canned diced green chile peppers
1 tablespoon	fresh cilantro minced
½ teaspoon	coarsely ground black pepper
¼ teaspoon	garlic powder
¼ teaspoon	seasoned salt
2 tablespoons	non-fat ranch salad dressing
½ teaspoon	Tabasco sauce
4	hamburger buns split and toasted

DIRECTIONS

1. In a large bowl, combine all ingredients, except buns; shape into 4 patties.

2. Place the burgers on the preheated grill and cook for 6 minutes or until meat thermometer inserted into center registers 170°F.

3. Place each patty on a bun and serve with condiments of your choice.

Plates needed: Grilling Plates
Preheat temperature: High
Estimated cooking time: 8 minutes

servings **4**

Grilled Garnet Sweet Potatoes with Fruit and Spiced Butter

INGREDIENTS

¼ cup	low-fat margarine melted
½ teaspoon	ground cinnamon
½ teaspoon	ground nutmeg
2	garnet sweet potatoes peeled and cut into ¼-inch slices
1	sweet orange peeled and thinly sliced
½ cup	fresh or canned pineapple cut into large chunks

DIRECTIONS

1. In a small bowl, combine margarine, cinnamon and nutmeg.

2. Place the sweet potato slices on the preheated grill in a single layer and cook for 5 minutes.

3. Place the orange slices on the sweet potatoes and arrange the pineapple chunks around the sides. Drizzle the spiced butter over all and continue cooking for 2 to 3 minutes.

POINTS

Grilled Potato and Garlic Salad

INGREDIENTS

4	**small red potatoes** cut into ¼-inch thick slices
1 teaspoon	**extra-virgin olive oil**
1 teaspoon	**dried basil**
1 teaspoon	**dried oregano**
1 teaspoon	**dried thyme**
10	**whole garlic cloves** peeled
½ teaspoon	**salt**
¼ teaspoon	**black pepper**
4 tablespoons	**non-fat mayonnaise**
1 tablespoon	**non-fat sour cream**
½ teaspoon	**Dijon mustard**
2 tablespoons	**capers**
1 teaspoon	**red wine vinegar**
1 teaspoon	**water**
1	**green onion** sliced
¼ cup	**fresh parsley** minced
2	**hard-cooked eggs** chopped

DIRECTIONS

1. In a small bowl, combine potato slices, oil, basil, oregano, thyme and garlic cloves; toss to coat. Place potato mixture on the baking plate in a single layer and cook for 7 minutes or until potatoes are tender.

2. Remove the garlic and peel.

3. In a small bowl, mash the grilled garlic with the salt and pepper. Blend in mayonnaise, sour cream, mustard, capers, vinegar, and water.

4. In a large bowl, combine potatoes, onion and parsley; add the eggs. Add the dressing and stir gently to mix.

5. Refrigerate for 1 hour to allow the flavors to blend.

ENTREES

Plates needed: Top Grilling Plate; Bottom Bake Plate
Preheat temperature: High
Estimated cooking time: 8-9 minutes

servings **4**

Yukon Ranch Potatoes

INGREDIENTS

4	**medium Yukon Gold potatoes** cut into ¼-inch thick cubes
½	**small green bell pepper** diced
½	**small red bell pepper** diced
½	**small onion** diced
2	**strips uncooked lean bacon** diced
1 tablespoon	**fresh parsley** minced
2 teaspoons	**seasoned salt**

DIRECTIONS

1. In a medium bowl, combine potatoes, peppers, onion, bacon, parsley and seasoned salt; toss well to mix.

2. Place the potato mixture in a single layer in the preheated baking plate and cook for 6 minutes, or until potatoes are tender and lightly browned.

3. Use a heat-resistant plastic spatula to turn and stir the potatoes at least once while cooking.

POINTS

CHOCOLATE CHIP
COOKIES
page 75

GRILLED
APPLE
PECAN CUPS
page 76

RUSTIC CHOCOLATE
PANINI page 80 ⌄

Chocolate Chip Cookies

INGREDIENTS

2 ½ cups	unsifted all-purpose flour
1 teaspoon	baking soda
1 cup	low-fat margarine softened
¾ cup	brown sugar firmly packed
½ cup	granulated sugar
2	eggs
1 teaspoon	vanilla extract
1	package semi-sweet chocolate chip morsels 12 ounces

DIRECTIONS

1. In a medium bowl, mix together the flour and baking soda.

2. In a large bowl, combine margarine and sugars and beat with an electric mixer at medium speed until light and fluffy.

3. Add the eggs and vanilla to the large bowl, and beat until blended, scraping sides of the bowl occasionally.

4. Beat in as much flour as possible with the mixer. Stir in remaining flour and chocolate morsels.

5. Drop the cookies by teaspoons, 2 inches apart, in the preheated baking plate and flatten the top of each cookie by pressing down with the back of a spoon.

6. Bake the cookies for 6 minutes per batch or until edges are firm.

7. Remove from baking plate and cool on wire rack.

8. Repeat with the remaining cookie dough or freeze remaining dough to bake later.

Tip from the Playbook

#1. Sweeten your Victory Lap with DESSERT

See photo on page 72

POINTS

Grilled Apple Pecan Cups

INGREDIENTS

2	**small baking apples** peeled and cored
¼ cup	**clover honey**
2 tablespoons	**pecans** chopped
1 tablespoon	**brown sugar**

DIRECTIONS

1. Cut the apples in half widthwise; scoop out the core and seeds.

2. Place a tablespoon of honey in the center of each apple half; add pecans and sprinkle with sugar.

3. Place the apples, cut side up, in the preheated baking plate and cook for 3 minutes or until heated through and softened.

4. If desired, serve topped with frozen low-fat vanilla yogurt or lemon sorbet.

Se
on

Hawaiian Pineapple Slices

INGREDIENTS

1 **fresh pineapple**
peeled and cored

¼ cup **clover honey**

1 teaspoon **ground cinnamon**

DIRECTIONS

1. Slice the pineapple into ¾–inch slices.
2. In a small bowl, combine honey and cinnamon.
3. Place the slices in a single layer on the preheated grill and drizzle the honey mixture over the slices.
4. Cook 3 minutes or until the pineapple is lightly browned.
5. Repeat with any remaining slices.
6. If desired, serve with raspberry or strawberry sorbet.

7
POINTS

Plates needed: Grilling Plates
Preheat temperature: Medium
Estimated cooking time: 2 minutes

Tiramisu

INGREDIENTS

2 cups	Mascarpone cheese
½ cup	powdered sugar
¼ cup	espresso powder
2 tablespoons	cocoa powder
½ cup	prepared low-fat vanilla pudding
4	slices pound cake cut 1-inch thick
¼ cup	strong black coffee
1 cup	non-fat whipped topping

DIRECTIONS

1. In a medium bowl, combine Mascarpone, sugar, espresso powder, 2 tablespoons of cocoa powder and vanilla pudding; mix well to blend.

2. Very lightly brush one side of each slice of cake with the coffee.

3. Spread a layer of the Mascarpone mixture on 2 slices of the cake, leaving a space around the edges. Cover each with a second slice of cake.

4. Place on preheated grill and cook for 2 minutes or until cake is lightly browned.

5. Top with the remaining Mascarpone mixture, whipped topping and sprinkle with additional cocoa powder.

Plates needed: Grilling Plates
Preheat temperature: Medium
Estimated cooking time: 2 minutes

Grilled Tropical Trifle

INGREDIENTS

4 slices angel food cake
cut 1-inch thick

4 slices fresh pineapple
cut ½-inch thick

1 banana
peeled and cut into
bite size pieces

**1 package sugar free
low calorie
vanilla pudding**
prepared according
to package directions
8 ounces

1 mango
thinly sliced

2 kiwi
peeled and thinly sliced

4 teaspoons coconut
shredded

4 teaspoons macadamia nuts
chopped

DIRECTIONS

1. Place the angel food cake slices on the preheated grill plate and cook for 2 minutes or until lightly browned.

2. Remove cake slices and place the pineapple on the grill plate; cook for 2 minutes.

3. In a medium bowl, mix the banana with the vanilla pudding.

4. To serve, place a pineapple slice on a dessert plate and top with 1 slice of grilled cake.

5. Spoon ½-cup banana pudding over each slice of cake and arrange the mango and kiwi slices on top in a fan shape, alternating the mango and kiwi.

6. Sprinkle with shredded coconut and nuts.

Rustic Chocolate Panini

INGREDIENTS

4	slices rustic French bread cut ½-inch thick
4 teaspoons	low-fat margarine
3 ounces	semi-sweet chocolate chips

DIRECTIONS

1. Spread the margarine on one side of each slice of bread and place buttered side down on a clean surface.

2. Top 2 slices of bread with half of the chips, leaving about ½-inch around the edges. Cover with a second slice of bread, buttered side up.

3. Place the panini on the preheated grill plate.

4. Cook for 2 minutes or until the chocolate is melted.

5. Cool slightly before serving and cut in half.

Tip: For variety, use white chocolate, dark chocolate or butterscotch chips!

See photo on page 74

Plates needed: Grilling Plates
Preheat temperature: Medium
Estimated cooking time: 2 minutes

Orange Cinnamon-Raisin Panini

INGREDIENTS

4 ounces	low-fat cream cheese
1 tablespoon	dark brown sugar
½ teaspoon	almond extract
4	slices cinnamon raisin bread cut ½-inch thick
1	large orange peeled and sliced
4 teaspoons	low-fat margarine

DIRECTIONS

1. In a small bowl, combine cream cheese, sugar and almond extract; mix well to blend.

2. Spread the margarine on one side of each slice of bread and place buttered side down on a clean surface.

3. Spread a layer of the cream cheese mixture on each of the 4 bread slices.

4. Place the orange slices on top of the cream cheese on 2 slices of bread and cover each with a second slice of bread, buttered side up.

5. Place the panini on the preheated grill plate.

6. Cook for 2 minutes or until the cream cheese is warm and the outside is golden brown.

7. Cool slightly and cut in half before serving.

POINTS

Plates needed: Grilling Plates
Preheat temperature: Medium
Estimated cooking time: 2 minutes

Chai Banana Shortcake

INGREDIENTS

2	**ripe bananas** peeled
¼ cup	**fresh orange juice**
1 teaspoon	**orange zest** finely grated
2 tablespoons	**dark brown sugar**
¼ teaspoon	**ground cardamom**
¼ teaspoon	**ground cinnamon**
⅛ teaspoon	**ground ginger**
2 tablespoons	**toasted pecans** chopped
4	**packaged shortcakes** substitute 4 slices low-fat pound cake
1 cup	**non-fat whipped topping**

DIRECTIONS

1. Cut the bananas in half horizontally.

2. In a small bowl, combine orange juice, orange zest, brown sugar, cardamom, cinnamon, ginger and pecans.

3. Place the bananas on the preheated grill plate and liberally spoon the mixture down the center of each banana half.

4. Cook for 2 minutes or until the bananas are softened and lightly browned.

5. To serve, place the shortcake on individual plates.

6. Cut the banana slices in half and place 2 pieces on top of each shortcake.

7. Drizzle with any glaze that has melted into the drip tray during cooking and garnish with whipped topping.

NOTES

NOTES